Praise for *Diggir*

'Thought-provoking and well written.
Peter R, Amazon.co.uk

'Shows what zest can be added to our garden reading.'
Helen Gazeley, Weeding the Web

'Cuts right through to the heart of the important issues that
mainstream garden lifestyle writers simply don't address.'
J. Ferguson, Amazon.co.uk

'An intelligent reminder of the joys and responsibilities
of gardening.'
Jebby7, Amazon.co.uk

'There is lots of humour.'
Cherry Lavell, Gloucestershire Organic Gardening Group

'Would like to see some more of his gardening wisdom.'
Savvyshopper, Amazon.co.uk

'An authentic voice in an often dull crowd of garden writing.'
Darren Lerigo, Modern Mint

'Everyone who professes to care about the world we live in
should read this book.'
Nicky Kyle, www.nickykylegardening.co.uk

'John Walker's prose makes for enjoyable reading.'
Nicholas Dakin-Elliot, Amazon.co.uk

'A very thought-provoking book which I enjoyed very much.'
Valerie Fairbank, Amazon.co.uk

'These essays are more relevant now than ever.'
Judith Conroy, Amazon.co.uk

DIGGING DEEP
in the garden

BOOK FOUR

John Walker

**Winner of the Garden Media Guild
Environmental Award**

Earth-friendly Books
www.earthfriendlygardener.net

For Richard Ellis

Copyright © 2016 by John Walker

ISBN: 978-0-9932683-7-3

Editor: Gaby Bartai

Cover design by Darren Moseley at Kablooie Creative

First published in the United Kingdom in 2016 (1)

Earth-friendly Books
Dolwyddelan
Snowdonia
North Wales

www.earthfriendlygardener.net

Cover image: Small copper butterfly (*Lycaena phlaeas*) on
poached egg plant (*Limnanthes douglasii*). Cover and
author image © John Walker

CONTENTS

INTRODUCTION

The essays in this fourth and final collection from my 'Digging Deep' column were originally published in *Kitchen Garden* magazine (which inherited the column after the demise of *Organic Gardening/Organic Garden & Home*). Although their flavour tilted toward a readership whose primary interest was growing food, they stayed true to the column's original goal: tackling the difficult and mostly unasked questions about how we gardeners (organic and earth-friendly, or otherwise) relate to broader environmental concerns, and how, in our gardening practices, we respond to them. I held true to the column's founding promise to 'rattle a few cages' – even bagging an award for doing so along the way.

I also bagged a fair amount of flak, some of it vituperative and, on occasion, bordering on the unhinged. What a jolly lot a tiny minority of that magazine's readers were; I never imagined that folk with a professed deep love of growing their own produce could hurl such bitter, vitriolic fruits. But some cages (fruit ones, perhaps) were thoroughly rattled, so my words duly kept their promise. This shone a revealing light on just how virulent some diehard and damaging gardening habits and attitudes still are, when – in times of mounting ecological turmoil – we need all the organic and nature-friendly gardening impetus we can get. Mercifully, those surprisingly bitter fruits came from a generation now in their own autumn phase.

But that wasn't the only surprise. After a few months of

plying the pages of *Kitchen Garden*, my words became worthy of their own curious disclaimer. 'John's views do not necessarily reflect those of the magazine' appeared whenever I explored apparently contentious topics – such as mooting the idea that frugal, more mindful organic gardening is the natural antidote to the over-consuming, resource-hungry 'normal' style of gardening sold by an industry desperately out of kilter with nature. I'd clearly scared the horses (ridden, no doubt, by jittery advertisers) sufficiently that the magazine felt it necessary to dissociate itself from my attempts to foster thoughtful debate around difficult issues. I guess I should have seen it coming. But, with hindsight, my words once again kept their promise.

The issues tackled in these essays are even more pressing today. Now more than ever, we gardeners need to dig, to delve, to ask and keep on asking challenging questions, both of ourselves and of gardening's status quo – and to keep those cages rattling.

Don't ever stop digging.

John Walker – Snowdonia, North Wales, Autumn 2016

DISCOMFORT ZONE

MY LAST GARDEN was a thin, narrow strip, typical of the kind found behind older terraced houses. Much to my chagrin, the prospect of gardening there (I wanted to do more than mow grass and sit on cheap and cheerless plastic chairs) came to fill me with dread. It was more buttock than cheek by jowl – and that was just with the neighbours' dog.

I was compelled, usually when I was trying to get on, to make neighbourly small talk, frequently through gritted teeth. Net curtains twitched and I felt the perpetual, burning inquisitiveness of curious eyes. Despite sustained attempts to convince myself that I could create an edible paradise there, I grew to hate my new garden and its horrible nakedness, so I never did discover how stuff fared.

So I got myself an allotment, just across the road. The most perfect and blissful thing about it was being there when everyone else had eventually gone home, usually on fine summer evenings.

By now you might have guessed that I'm a bit of a solitary soul when it comes to gardening. My current patch is at the end of an unmade track, the nearest neighbours are several hundred metres away (in summer they're completely blotted out by greenery), and I don't have to crave summer evenings any more. My garden starts a few metres from my front door and I can nip out into it any time, with the risk of no more than a cheery 'hello' from a rare perambulator on the footpath. Most days I eyeball more buzzards, jays and dragonflies than I do *Homo sapiens*. Bliss.

I find it hard to be the model 'neighbourly' sort. I wouldn't dream of poking my nose into my neighbours' business, unless I thought they needed help – or they asked for it. Worse still, I'm lousy at being, or even feeling, part of a – here comes the word that's guaranteed to bring me out in a cold sweat, even inside my wellies – 'community'.

Just as I'm not the neighbourly sort, nor am I the community sort. Maybe it's the way I was brought up, but I just don't feel comfortable doing the touchy-feely, huggy, let's-work-together, dreadlocks, groupy – add to the list as you wish – community 'thing'. I've tried, and felt like a fish taking its final gasp. I might be painting something of a caricature, but it's a painfully accurate one, and I find the notion of 'community' all the more unappealing when, however good the intentions, its template is overlaid on to gardening.

I know from studying permaculture, where hugs are mandatory, that pushing out our personal 'comfort zone' is supposed to be liberating and empowering; on my plot all I want to push is my wheelbarrow. At the risk of sounding politically as well as increasingly horticulturally incorrect, I'll stick my head up from behind the compost bin and say that the very idea of 'community gardening' sends a shiver down my spine. It can't just be me; how are your vertebrae doing?

But it's *de rigueur* that we should now all be gardening together, growing side by side in togetherness as part of a green-fingered community. The nation's 'head gardener', Toby Buckland, declared at the start of the current series of BBC TV's 'Gardeners' World' that we are "in this together". Yuk.

Cornwall's media-savvy Eden Project got out its touchy-feelies recently with its 'The Big Lunch' campaign, which set aside a Sunday in July as a 'day to break bread with our neighbours, to put a smile on Britain's face. The food, entertainment and decorations we will have either grown, cooked, or created ourselves.' Thank goodness nothing came up when I typed in my postcode; I've seen some alarming pictures. One 'big lunch' seemed to consist of beer, burnt bangers, bread rolls and, more optimistically, a few home-grown salads.

This month sees the Royal Horticultural Society (RHS) event 'Dig together day: unearthing the nation's gardening knowledge', which is billed as 'a nationwide celebration and awareness-raising day for gardening clubs and horticultural societies... an opportunity for clubs, groups and societies across the UK to open their doors and invite members of their community to come along, find out more about what they do and perhaps even learn some new gardening skills... the whole idea is to work together to create a great community gardening event.' My vertebrae are all a-tingle.

I think one of the reasons I get so much out of gardening, especially growing food, is that my gardens and allotments have always been sanctuaries from a society that, no matter how hard it tries, still mostly only manages to talk the talk on community. It's a lovely soft-focus notion that we're all somehow 'pulling together' as a human family, but reality tends to tell a different story; decades of social fragmentation coupled with rampant materialism are, like knotted twine, gonna take some unpicking.

So rather than dabbling in a bit of well-meant social re-engineering, whose premise is that we'll all be enriched if we get to know each other better and rekindle 'community' spirit, why not encourage folk, whatever size their comfort zone, to just get on with it? Let them work quietly, discreetly, on their own; I know that I get my most productive gardening done working solo. Don't let's get distracted from the fact that it's the gardening that's important; kitchen gardening, especially, brings significant environmental benefits.

I constantly need to check on stuff like sowing times, and I like to keep abreast of new plants and growing techniques, and of wider environmental thinking and debate. All of this helps me to constantly reassess whether what I'm doing in my garden is as earth-friendly as it can be, but it's not group work. I learnt my basic gardening skills many moons back, but today, with the amount of gardening information available from either a paper or a virtual page, or from TV and the internet, I doubt that I'd actually need my college days over again. Even if I was starting from scratch, I just don't think I'd get what I need from being part of a 'community'.

If we look at kitchen gardening through an environmental lens, it's blindingly obvious that it's imperative to get more and more people growing as much of their own food as possible. Growing our own organically cuts food miles, shrinks water footprints, slashes packaging, improves health, negates the need for resource-hungry garden chemicals and fertilisers, boosts biodiversity and, as Garden Organic's research has shown, substantially reduces our carbon footprints. Less carbon dioxide going into our atmosphere means we might just spare future generations the full wrath of climate breakdown.

If those organisations currently flogging their community gardening credentials put as much energy into promoting home food-growing as a serious, can-do way of creating self-reliance, as they are into getting us all dancing in the streets, we'd be flying the low-carbon flag at full mast.

We need to decide where our priorities are. Does it really make sense, with our biosphere in crisis, to be pouring so much effort into rebuilding how we relate to each other, when we have climate change threatening to tear apart the planetary community that is life itself?

Blimey, I think I need a hug.

October 2009

GOING WITH MY GUTS

THE NEXT THOUSAND WORDS or so are going to be a bit of a gamble, but if, like me, you're well and truly cheesed off with the game of ping-pong that's recently broken out over the merits (or otherwise) of organic food, it will hopefully be worth it.

This game is one of words, and the 'ball' in play has 'nutrition' and 'health benefits' emblazoned all over it. The key players are the Food Standards Agency (FSA), an independent government department set up 'to protect the public's health and consumer interests in relation to food', and the Soil Association, 'the UK's leading organic organisation [who] promote planet-friendly food and farming'. Other players have been pitching in too, including the 'meeja', with its usual in-depth and incisive news analysis intended for all those with a 30-second (or shorter) attention span.

In a predictably depressing manner, the 'debate' has focused largely on the spat that's broken out following publication of the FSA's review of organic food, which found that '... there is little, if any, nutritional difference between organic and conventionally produced food and there is no evidence of additional health benefits from eating organic food.' The FSA review, carried out by the London School of Hygiene and Tropical Medicine, looked at '... all papers published over the past 50 years that related to the nutrient content and health differences between organic and conventional food.'

The anti-organic brigade has had a field day. Our pro-chemical punditocracy, including those in the gardening media, have been busy dusting off their long and wearied lists of reasons to ditch earth-friendly organic gardening, as they urge us all to switch to 'conventional' gardening. What's the point of it, they gleefully argue, if the government is telling us there's no benefit in eating organic food? – better to offload organic and garden 'properly'. Some have been harebrained enough to suggest we should shove nature aside while we get to grips with gardening (especially food growing, they say) – we should bring on the chemical corps, then go back to the hard drudge of gardening organically later on, if we really must, once everything has been knocked into shape.

My response is, sadly, unprintable on these hallowed pages, but I can tell you that it was preceded by my baying with anger among my runner beans, and followed by a long sigh of frustrated despair.

But what this reinvigorated debate has done is to get me thinking more than ever before about exactly why I grow, buy and eat organic food. The papers included in the FSA review were almost certainly the result of scientific analysis, resulting from experiments and research conducted by the white-coated inhabitants of laboratories, the haunts of scientific rigour. All will have focused on very specific, narrow criteria – in this case differences in nutrient levels and the perceived health benefits of eating organic versus non-organic food. And in doing so, they will, naturally, have left out so much.

But that's what I'm interested in – what the boffins in white coats can't find, pin down, label, measure or even identify, that something, that feeling, that palpable aura about home-grown organic food that defies scientific investigation or analysis. For me it's the ungraspable dimension of gardening organically that keeps me strong in my belief that it's simply the right thing to do in a world that's seriously overstepping its environmental limits. I don't think I actually care much whether organic food is better for me nutritionally; the humble act of simply growing it gives me more 'benefits' than any test tube-gazing scientist can track down, and they're not all related to what passes down my oesophagus. For me, it's about not just what goes into my guts, but what my guts are telling me. I did say this was going to be a gamble.

So here I am, bereft of white coat, devoid of test tubes, offering you nothing in the way of peer-reviewed science published in some august, internationally-respected journal. But the one thing I do have, of sorts, is a laboratory – it's called my garden. I don't carry out strictly scientific experiments there, but a lot of experimentation, teaching and research goes on, although audio-visual gizmos and microscopes are absent, and nature is head tutor. Whether I'm squishing cabbage caterpillars, watching two weasels scrap as they weave in and out of my slate walls, or gathering a colander of fresh veg within sight of my kitchen, I'm acutely aware that my 'gardenlab' is much more than a lab: it's a green-hued crucible of ideas, thoughts and, perhaps above all else, feelings.

Please don't run away at this point. Feelings are important to us organic gardeners, and surely none experience such deep and meaningful ones as those of us who choose to make that most fundamental of all gestures, that of growing food to feed ourselves. One of my favourite feelings is the one I get when I 'plug into' the earth. Imagining my hand as equivalent to a plug going into a socket, and with eyes closed, I envisage myself as the tiniest of specks, wondrously connected to gardens, and indeed to the whole of nature, via a powerful global web of interconnected roots. That'll get the pro-chemical pundits spluttering into their sprayers.

Unplugged, and back to tending my own intimate patch, growing my own food brings myriad other feelings: joy at the sheer abundance of life that my garden encourages, whether it's lizards basking on the slates I've left among the long grass, or a haze of hoverflies vying for a slot on the marigolds amongst my tomatoes; awe at how tiger worms turn every scrap of rottable material into rich, energising compost; amazement at how the reddish, nutrient-poor soil that once anchored tall stands of bracken is slowly darkening as worms and compost work their alchemy; reassurance in the knowledge that most of what I eat contains no unnatural chemical residues, and that if the shops run dry, I'll have something to eat; and humility at how my garden gets me thinking. It increasingly challenges and informs the way I see the world, and paints me an unfolding picture of how we'll all need to be gardening – and living – in the not too distant future.

These are just a few of my favourite feelings. Together, they make me feel good – good about myself, and good about my place on an imperfect and increasingly ecologically embattled planet. If that's not a 'health benefit', I don't know what is.

The act of growing food organically nourishes me as much as the food itself, and that's something which no FSA review or scientific report into the 'benefits' of organic food – nor the one-dimensional arguments that follow – can ever finger. And that, surely, is a good thing. Just like when I plug into my soil, there's something hugely liberating in knowing that there are some unfathomable things which can outmanoeuvre the yapping hounds of sometimes dubiously motivated science.

It might be just a feeling deep down in my guts, but it's a mightily empowering one.

November 2009

AHEAD OF THE CARBON CURVE

YOU KNOW, I'M SURE THE WORMS in my compost bin have got a sense of humour. Now there's a slight risk that I might be imagining this, but a little while back, after consigning a front page of the *Daily Mail* to composting nirvana, I'm pretty positive my bin rocked with the hearty cackles of its segmented annelid inhabitants.

They must be laughing a lot of the time – not just when a holed pair of my organic cotton underpants (only the best for my worms) lands in their laps. Each fresh delivery from my compost caddy brings them evidence of our profligate use of resources, as cereal packets, card food packaging, tea bags, scrunched cardboard, envelopes, newspapers, and anything else of organic origin that will (or sometimes won't) rot away, rain down on these eager compost-creators.

Coverage of even the most fundamental and pressing environmental issues is, as a rule, given short, superficial shrift in our tabloid newspapers; the *modus operandi* of these publications (apart from being useful compost material) is to provide sensationalist headlines that reassure the great washed that environmental concern equates to an attack on their readers' freedom. One such story had my worms sliding over themselves with laughter.

'A slop bucket for every home', yelled the *Daily Mail*. 'Ministers plan to impose fines if you don't recycle food waste.' Shock, horror. The government is planning to reduce some of the mountain of food waste that goes to landfill each year in the UK, which, when mixed with everything else we bury out of sight and mind, produces, amongst other insidious pollutants, methane, a global warming gas 20 times more potent than carbon dioxide (CO_2). It is currently investigating whether food waste can be collected and redeployed away from our traditional 'dump and forget' waste streams.

As the worms' laughter subsided and they munched their way merrily through the words 'slop bucket', headlines flashed of an altogether more intelligent but also more disquieting nature: we're losing 2.2 million tonnes of the UK's topsoil each year, mostly through erosion by wind and rain. Our emaciated farmland and forest soils, starved of organic matter, are blowing and washing away. A government study has identified the root causes, unsurprisingly, as intensive farming and industrial pollution. This is doubtless mirrored in gardens and allotments across the land; chemical- and fertiliser-addicted gardening knocks the stuffing out of that thin, life-giving layer of brown stuff, just like feed-the-plants, forget-the-soil farming has done.

What's ringing alarm bells at the Department for Environment, Food and Rural Affairs (Defra) is concern over how the UK is going to feed itself in the future. With our agricultural soils in a dire state, the prognosis for increasing the amount of food we grow as a nation isn't looking good.

Defra estimates that our soils lock away ('sequester', in boffin-speak) around 10 billion tonnes of carbon (half of it in peat bogs), with huge potential for it to lock up even more. And just as my worms burped after swallowing the last bits of the *Daily Mail*, along came another, more deeply worrying headline, this time from the Met Office, warning of 'catastrophic global warming in our lifetimes'.

Scientific estimates tend to psychologically shunt the effects of severe climate change off into the yet-to-be-lived lives of future generations, but new research from climatologists is bringing us down to earth with a bump. Our fossil fuel-driven lives (which show no sign of abating) could mean that folk alive today might well witness, following a 4°C rise in temperature, the loss of up to half of the planet's species, threats to the water supplies of half the world's population, and the swamping of low-lying coastal communities. If you plan on being around in 2060, take note; there's a real chance you'll witness this planetary fever for yourself.

One increasingly important strand of thought as to how we might still avert climate breakdown (apart from drastically reducing CO_2 emissions) is to find ways of removing the carbon that's already there. One of the best and easiest ways, as soil scientists will tell you, is to add composted organic matter to the soil, and practice 'minimum tillage'.

In gardening speak, that means making compost as if our biosphere's health depended on it, and avoiding the annual ritual of chopping up that precious skin of soil, on which our very existence depends. When you dig soil, you not only turn a fragile ecosystem repeatedly on its head, you expose the soil to the air, which turns organic matter to CO_2. This drifts away unseen, helping to ease up the global thermostat. Hold on to your cloth caps, but we are no longer in the age of the spade.

If the government does go ahead with its plans to collect food waste, I'll be declining its offer of a 'slop bucket'. On the rare occasions that I 'waste' food, it goes straight into the compost caddy and then into my compost bin. 'Slop' is anathema here, and I'm not big on bins. I have no wheelie bin. Not possessing one of these malodorous vessels of our 'dump and forget' mentality helps to tune you out of throwaway thinking, and into 'can I compost it?' awareness. Only if the worms can't turn it into energised, soil-building compost, and it can't be recycled, does any waste get, reluctantly, thrown away. A vegetarian diet spares you the dilemma of what to do with bones – even steely tiger worms find those tough going.

So there's one alarmist headline sorted: rather than spend zillions foisting a 'slop collection' system on a reluctant public, why not explain how to turn 'slops', along with all the garden 'waste' (aka valuable resource) that they religiously ram into their brown wheelie bin, into a rich, ultra-local soil food?

Cue the laughing boys. Fast-moving, red and thrashing composting worms will find a bin wherever you put it, and will soon turn all of your garden and kitchen 'waste', plus a good deal else (including tabloid newspapers) into rich, worm-worked organic compost. Adding this to your soil will grow you healthy, resilient and nutrient-rich crops, and even more importantly, as your soil becomes ever more enriched with organic matter, and remains as undisturbed as possible, it will be able to lock up increasing amounts of carbon.

Organic gardeners have been nurturing and improving soil for far longer than forget-the-soil farmers and gardeners have been abusing it, so we can greet government headlines about vanishing soils with a philosophical shrug. But the realisation that the soil in our gardens and allotments, if we care for it mindfully, might help us do our bit toward staving off climate breakdown, brings added gusto to our determination to garden in not just an earth-friendly way, but an earth-cooling one.

In December, bods from 200 countries will attend the 15th meeting of the parties to the United Nations Framework Convention on Climate Change. The outcome of this mega-meeting will test whether humanity can pull together to avert changes to our climate that will affect every species on earth, from humans to composting worms. Who'd have thought that we organic gardeners would be ahead of the curve when it comes to cutting carbon?

Now there's a headline that's truly sensational.

December 2009

NO PURCHASE NECESSARY

AM I THE ONLY organic gardener who finds a visit to a garden centre, especially at this time of year, an uncomfortable and unsettling experience? The very phrase 'garden centre' is something of a misnomer, at least as far as the word 'garden' is concerned, especially in the case of the megastores. Once you've tossed the tinsel aside, navigated the bauble-fest, and plotted a safe route through the artificial snow to bypass Santa's grotto, you might just stumble back into the 'gardening' zone. If it weren't for the saving grace of a few green leaves (albeit of some dismal evergreen shrub) you might be forgiven for thinking that you'd strayed into just another glittering shrine to Western consumerism.

Fortunately, we organic gardeners with a food-growing flair are more adept than most at cutting a path through the tat in these temples of temptation; we generally know what we want and we know that earth-friendly organic gardening is essentially a buy-very-little activity. I bet the watchers of the CCTV screens in these soulless supercentres can spot an 'organic' a mile off. We're the ones devoid of the fixed supermarket gaze of the zombified consumer (how else do they get through it?). The cameras will track us as we sweep past the chemical aisles, cast a discerning eye over anything dubiously labelled 'organic', frown at an overpriced (and imported) 'bee box', and head for the compost area. Over the last year, my own bit of garden centre consumption has consisted almost entirely of buying peat-free compost and grabbing a cup of tea (I gave the cameras a parting wink).

The truth is that organic gardeners are bad news for establishments where the prime objective is to keep the tills a-bleeping. You could say we're also bad news for the economy – but only if you subscribe to the myth that economic growth is the only game in town, and that it can continue unbridled on a planet with finite natural resources. The flip side, of course, is that we organic gardeners are simply off the scale when it comes to having a positive impact on the world around us. We know all about working with nature and respecting its limits, and we feed ourselves.

Think about it: we're being bombarded day in and day out with messages telling us that to really 'go green' costs money (think solar panels, home insulation, hybrid cars), and yet as organic gardeners we tend to spend less as our resolve deepens. The better and savvier we become at growing organically, the deeper green we become. We could, perhaps, even puff out our muddy chests and claim to be the 'original' shade of green.

Every time we buy something we send a small but powerful signal down the supply line that tells someone that we wanted it – and that we probably want more of it. We create a demand which sets off a whole chain reaction of events, from the manufacture of whatever it is that we're indicating we want, to its packaging, marketing, transportation and sale. As it gears up to meet that signal of demand, each link in the chain starts to suck in both energy and resources.

Last summer, aphids decided to make a picnic out of my sweet potatoes. For about a week I managed to contain their antics, by squidging them between finger and thumb, but then I dropped my guard for a few days. Despite vain blasts of eco-friendly washing-up liquid, the population exploded, and I was squidged out. But just as desperation set in, the hoverflies turned up, lured by nearby pot marigolds. I watched, mesmerised, as they quietly and methodically laid eggs among the sap-sucking hordes. Within a week the hoverflies' larvae had cleaned up. Job done, not a penny spent, and no signal of demand sent out. The only energy required was in making a mental note to renew my faith in nature.

Losing my bottle and reaching for an insecticide would, naturally, have sent out a very different message. If I'd plumped for one of the ready-to-use sprays (just point and squirt), I would effectively have been grasping a dollop of oil; the plastic container, and most synthetic pesticides and fungicides, are, essentially, made from crude oil, a finite natural resource.

The resulting bleep at the garden centre checkout would have sent the signal off down the wires to head office, and thenceforth on down the supply line until it finally reached the chemical manufacturing plant (located who knows where). On receipt of the signal, more oil would have been called up for making the next ready-to-use bug spray. Meanwhile, more energy, derived from burning finite fossil fuels such as coal and gas – whose pollutant emissions are causing global warming – would have been used both to make the spray and to power up the entire supply chain.

Let's not forget that extracting the raw materials to sate the signal of demand comes with its own set of associated dangers – from oil spills and water and air pollution to the irreparable destruction of our landscapes. And what are conditions like for the workers on the production line at the factory where the bug spray is made? Do they enjoy the same levels of employment protection and safety at work as we take for granted? You'll have a hard time tracking down a bottle of a man-made garden chemical carrying a 'fairtrade' symbol.

Looked at this way, mainstream gardening doesn't seem quite as 'green' as we're increasingly being told it is – told, that is, by the garden centres themselves (not to mention their insidious televised equivalents). You'll hear a lot in the coming years about just how 'green' garden centres (and the gardening industry) are. Judging by the noises coming from recent gatherings of the great and the good of the garden trade, they'll be selling their eco-credentials hard – no matter how illusory they are.

My advice is to take it all with a very big boulder of rock salt, and to think greenwash rather than green. Indeed, one chain, the Garden Centre Group (formerly Wyevale) has announced that it's ditching some of its environmental policies because it thinks it's green by default, and sees them as 'gimmicks'. Another, Dobbies, is busy building huge out-of-town retail temples accessible only by car, just when the world is realising that it might actually be rather a good idea if we started using our cars a little less. Remind me to give those temples a miss.

Food gardeners in particular need to be on their guard. The gardening industry is gearing up to cash in on the flourishing interest in kitchen gardening, and will be pulling out the stops to milk it for all it's worth.

As organic gardeners we're instinctively opposed to the unnecessary and the excessive. We prefer to engage with nature to keep our soil and plants in good health, to embrace thrift, and to utilise resources close to home, rather than rely on products emanating from way down a long chain of distant, unseen events over which we have no control.

Gardening organically might not do much to fatten profits, but it will give you sway over your plot's relationship with the wider world, and any demands you might be making on it. You might feel the occasional pang for a bout of garden retail therapy, but you can take heart from knowing that in the grand ecological scheme of things, less really is more.

January 2010

RESILIENCE GARDENING

BARBED WIRE AND BASEBALL BATS might not seem obvious topics to pepper a chat over a cuppa about kitchen gardening, but they're signposts that conversations with a food gardening friend seem to be following more and more. Ever since our first confab took the 'barbed wire route' a few years ago, our uplifting chinwags about how delicious the first earlies were, or how well the toms are doing, have been accompanied by a gathering sense of gloom. It's not what you'd expect of folk that get such a high out of growing things – we're not used to cultivating despondency.

The roots of all this 'barbed wire' talk reach back to the autumn of 2000, and the fuel protests, when lorry drivers, farmers and others blockaded UK oil refineries. For a few weeks it sent the country into topsy-turvy mode, as the growing threat to fuel supplies triggered panic buying at garage forecourts. The effect soon rippled out to shops and supermarkets, with several of the big stores cautioning that panic buying coupled with fuel shortages meant that there might only be enough food for a few days' supply. Supermarkets rationed staples like milk and bread. For a few bizarre days, civilisation started to dysfunction. Remember?

This shock to the country's infrastructure also threatened serious consequences for our health services, postal deliveries, manufacturing, national security, the transport network... but it was those images of supermarket shelves being cleared, amid a primeval feeding frenzy, that started to haunt our chinwags on the veg plot. All of what occurred in 2000 was symptomatic of what happens when you start, even gently, to pull the plug on an infrastructure that's almost totally reliant on an uninterrupted supply of the black stuff – oil. By choking off the supply of fossil fuels like petrol and diesel, a few otherwise upstanding citizens sent shockwaves through a way of life we take, increasingly at our peril, for granted.

You could almost feel the heat drain from our cups of tea on the day, during one natter on the plot, that we stepped over the line. We asked ourselves: what would have happened if the fuel protests had gone on for weeks, or even months? It makes my palms clammy just to write it.

My friend's organic kitchen garden is an extensive one, and is an integral part of her smallholding, with cattle, sheep, chickens and geese in the mix – as well as her family. She is a powerhouse of self-reliance, and with much hard work she makes self-sufficiency look attainable. Pondering the breakdown of everything we take for granted, and amid such abundance, I well remember getting to the killer thought before she did: where on earth will people go if the shops ever do run out of food?

Although we laughed over our steaming mugs at the time, the answer to my question – that they'd come up the lane in a mob, bash my friend, if she tried to stop them, over the head with a baseball bat, and take what vegetables, fruit and livestock they wanted – has since lost any comedic quality. Whether such a ravenous posse would actually know what to do with (or how to kill and prepare) what they'd looted is another story. Autumn 2000 showed that it only takes days for normal and generally rational people to succumb to those base survival instincts that lie deep in us all. Pushing and shoving in the supermarket aisles is one thing, but what would our psyches be like after weeks or months, stoked by that most powerful motivator, hunger?

The truth is that we live in a society that depends on an oil-addicted infrastructure that's as critical to the smooth running of everyday life as it is fragile and vulnerable to 'attack'. The frenzy of 2000 was triggered by a small number of disgruntled, determined citizens – not by a targeted terrorist attack on our country's 'normal life' support system.

It's comforting to think that those of us with decent-sized kitchen gardens or allotments might fare pretty well if 'normal life' took a dip for a while and our food shops temporarily locked their doors. With a bit of planning and forethought, we could get by without luxuries and even cut back on staples, making the most, depending on the season, of what could be picked either fresh from the garden, or got from the freezer or from store. But it's also fanciful thinking. Survival instincts are eventually going to trump any amount of barbed wire fencing, even if you've acquired your own baseball bat to defend your veggies, and allotments will offer rich pickings for insatiable mobs, making vandalism seem pale by comparison.

Some of these 'survival instincts' are already kicking in; the recession has sown the seeds of endless stories of how produce is being stolen, mostly from allotments, all over the country. This isn't wanton destruction, it's the spiriting away of entire crops, almost certainly fuelled by the felonious desperation of those struggling to keep pace with ever-escalating food prices.

The deep irony is that these real-life pilferers (as well as my fictional, bat-wielding mob) will probably be feasting on some of the most locally grown, chemical-free food they have ever eaten. Although changes are afoot in the way we feed ourselves as a nation, it's still a fact that for most people, food comes from a long way away, and is conveyed to them via a thundering, oil-dependent transport network that gets it there 'just in time'.

With climate change upon us, and the age of cheap, abundant

oil drawing to a close (expert opinion is converging on the consensus that we've already hit, or are about to reach, 'peak oil', after which supplies will gradually diminish), we face profound changes to the way our oil-soaked lives are shaped.

For kitchen gardeners, 'food supply chains' are non-existent. It's food feet (metres if you must) for us – but it's the long, global supply chains, powered by oil, that are the weak links in civilisation as we know it. Luckily, we're waking up to the realisation that the best way to stave off my bat-wielding mob is to drastically reduce the length (and vulnerability) of those supply chains.

That's what all the 'relocalisation' buzz is about. Bringing food production as close as possible to where it's consumed is one of the guiding tenets of the work being done by the Transition movement – a global network working to build resilience into communities as we face up to the twin threats of climate change and peak oil, as well as future economic uncertainty. Much Transition work is focused on trying to rebuild the local food networks that used to exist around most towns and cities (when 'local food' meant local food) in preparation for life in a post-oil, low-carbon world.

Organic gardeners are pretty low-oil gardeners by default. We're well-placed to play our part in rethinking and reshaping our nation's foodscape, so it can both withstand and quickly bounce back from whatever future shocks or traumas it might encounter. Quite simply, the more of us there are growing as much food as we possibly can, the less likely it is that I'll wake up from nightmares about baseball bats.

Our gardens and allotments, whatever their size, are making a priceless contribution, not just by cultivating a growing sense of self-reliance in us as we tend them, but also by cultivating resilience itself.

February 2010

STRANGE BEDFELLOWS

WITHOUT KNOWING QUITE where it's going, and with some reluctance, I recently parted with £28 of my hard-earned cash. The call-up for my twenty-eight quid was a subscription reminder from Garden Organic (GO), the UK's national charity for organic growing, of which I have been a member for many years.

What caused me to waver were still-gnawing doubts following the announcement last autumn that GO is proposing, imminently, to enter into a commercial partnership with Webbs Garden Centres Ltd (WGC), whose HQ is at Droitwich in Worcestershire. My conundrum is that for the first time ever I'm not sure whether my £28 is potentially going toward 'researching and promoting organic gardening, farming and food', or helping to expand the business interests of the ecologically indifferent gardening industry.

The reason for this proposed partnership, in which WGC takes over the running of the shop, cafe, restaurant and conference facilities at GO's HQ at Ryton, near Coventry, seems to be, in a nutshell, that GO is in dire financial straits, and has been for some time, for a whole potting shed full of interlocking reasons. A sense of desperation was palpable in the way news of the proposal was broken; the 30,000-plus GO members first heard of it via an announcement in the members-only section of the GO website, while everyone else had to wait until the story 'broke' in the horticultural trade press.

From the perspective of a GO member, the whole 'announcement' phase was a shambles, and you can still only read about the proposals if you access the members-only section of the GO website. There will still be members who don't know what is being mooted, because no one saw fit to ask their opinion; no one saw fit to write to them, using paper, envelope and stamp, to even tell them about it. That's not the way to engage with a loyal membership, some of whom have supported the organisation since it first drew breath.

Judging by some of the comments on GO's online forum, this total lack of consultation has gone down very badly. There have been stampings of feet, threats of resignation and calls for Extraordinary General Meetings – along with a few comments supportive of the proposed partnership and suggesting that GO members put their trust in 'the management'. All of this appears to have cut little ice with said management. There has been next to no online interaction with concerned members, apart from a hastily prepared 'Q&A' document, in which the originators got to choose both the questions and the answers (it was described by one member as a 'disgraceful set of managed questions'). Of course, it should have been the 30,000-plus members of GO who were asking the questions, not some anonymous entity trying to quell a self-induced revolt.

One of the great things about the 21st century is the abundance of ways in which people can link up to discuss and debate matters of shared concern, whether they're just around the corner or on the other side of the earth. Quite what stopped GO from being transparent and candid with its membership I don't know, but I do know it would have involved relatively little effort to establish an online forum dedicated to the discussion of a departure that, if it goes ahead, could taint the credibility of organic gardening for a long time to come.

Announcing the proposed arrangement, GO said that the move is designed to 'enable as many people as possible to enjoy organic and climate-friendly gardening', while WGC chipped in with 'we understand that many customers would prefer to garden chemical-free, especially those new to the activity'. Well, here's to that, but there's a whole heap more to climate-friendly organic gardening than just being 'chemical-free'. It's as much about adopting a philosophical, prudent approach to gardening as it is about not buying and using garden chemicals – or any of the other gardening paraphernalia that is relentlessly foisted upon us.

There's surely a painful rub in the offing when the organisation dedicated to researching and demonstrating organic practice at the back garden level jumps into bed with a profit-driven company whose *raison d'être* is to flog as much stuff as possible; frugality will, I guarantee, not be writ large in WGC's business plan. I find it hard to believe that no one within GO saw this particular bit of screeching discord coming, but dissenting voices are, perhaps, few. We organic gardeners are, by our very nature, a thrifty lot. We just don't buy much 'stuff', because earth-friendly gardening inherently requires a minimal 'take' from our planet's finite and rapidly depleting resources. Indeed, it gives plenty back to our embattled biosphere, and just by going about gardening organically we cultivate something inside ourselves, which results in the blooming of a greener state of mind.

GO will retain responsibility for its demonstration gardens at Ryton, and hope to 'inspire and educate' the increased number of visitors which it's assumed will follow the establishment of 'Webbs Ryton Gardens'. I wonder just how far these unlikely bedfellows are prepared to go in ensuring that the surge in visitors to Ryton doesn't lead to ballooning emissions from all the cars needed to get folk there. If you set yourself up as a visitor attraction, you need to shoulder at least some of the responsibility for the environmental impact of your fans – especially if you're promoting 'climate-friendly' gardening.

But perhaps what's most at risk of being lost is the very voice that GO can claim to speak with on matters organic – a voice of authority that's still authentic and which carries clout. Once a line is crossed, and GO starts signalling that organic gardening is just like all other gardening – something you increasingly buy rather than do – then its voice will grow weak and feeble. It will become part of a gardening industry that, despite what it professes publicly, sputters disdain at the very mention of anything to do with 'the environment'.

GO likes to present itself as a 'campaigning' body, but its efforts on that front have been lamentable in recent years, despite it being regularly pilloried by certain sections of the gardening media. If it signs this deal, GO is going to find the job of shining the light of sustainability on the wider gardening industry a whole lot harder; ideas of bottom-up 'greening', although admirable, will always be pie in the profit-driven sky.

I can't be the only one who's stumped up their £28 in good faith, but with nagging doubts about whether GO can sustain its mandate to walk the organic gardening talk if creeping commercialisation takes root. Although this move has been spun as a 'fabulous opportunity' to somehow 'green' the gardening industry by association, and to make it more sustainable from the checkouts up, I believe that if the protagonists do the deal (it isn't 'done' at the time of writing) then so very much risks being lost. It could turn out to be an act of sheer folly; one that could severely curtail the potential of earth-friendly organic gardening to play a much greater part in the more balanced, less overconsuming, more planet-friendly lives that we must all start living soon.

The current trajectory looks, to me at least, like a desperate stumbling backwards, rather than a creative leap forward in a fast-changing world.

March 2010

ELECTION SPECIAL

AMID FEVERED MEDIA SPECULATION about the date for the general election, I am as delighted as I am humbled to announce that I intend to stand for parliament, where I will sow the seeds of a dynamic new force in British politics. Fresh and forward-thinking, it will put real plot into politics, so that within a few short months of my party taking office, 'political plotting' will gain a new, historic meaning. When I say that my party will appeal to the grass roots, I truly mean it.

This new, vibrant and earth-centric powerhouse for change will be known as The Gardening Party (TGP). Its policies will be driven by the seriousness of the environmental challenges which lie ahead: the intertwined threats of climate change and 'peak oil', resource depletion, destruction of natural habitats, global pollution and the planet-wide erosion of biodiversity.

My party's ambitions will bring new hope to every corner of the earth where people are passionate about growing plants, especially to eat. Our far-reaching policies, some radical and revolutionary, are born of a dynamic crucible of green ideas into which has been poured the latest and best knowledge from organic, biodynamic and vegan-organic gardening, permaculture, and the horticultural, agricultural and social sciences. For some, hard and unpopular choices lie ahead. My 'big shed' will welcome input from all, but TGP's aim is to never again let the direction of our gardening nation be dictated by vested interests and self-interested celebrity.

We stand, my fellow kitchen gardeners, on an ecological precipice. Together we can join hands, step back from the edge of the abyss and into the glow of a new green dawn, and start cultivating ourselves a better, more resilient future. Will you, fellow plotters, gaze at the dirt under your fingernails, feel the untapped power of what you do in helping heal our damaged earth, and join me in nurturing a new and greener Britain?

The Gardening Government will introduce a deep green paper on our proposals to give every citizen a 'right to grow'. We will instigate research to establish how much land is required to offer everyone the level of self-sufficiency of their choosing. We will then legislate to ensure that all new homes are automatically allocated their own 'growplots'. These will be our nation's flexible, future allotments. Anyone not wanting a growplot can donate it to a pool of 'edible space' for their area, which will be used to help meet the ever-increasing demand for space to grow healthy, chemical-free food.

As part of our growplot programme, we will carry out a sweeping review of the carbon intensity of green space in towns and cities. Where fleets of ride-on mowers consume vast quantities of fuel just to cut the grass, we will bring about a transformation. We will replace the snarl of mowers with a network of integrated growplots producing an abundance of fresh, untravelled, seasonal and ultra-local organic food. These will be the community-owned and -tended market gardens of the 21st century. All gardeners will be offered a subsidised greenhouse or polytunnel, so they can play their part in our emerging and renewably-powered 'solar society'.

To fund the growplot programme and our other plans, and deter the most environmentally damaging gardening practices, my party's most immediate task will be to introduce a range of climate-friendly taxes. Garden chemicals and fertilisers derived from oil and other non-renewables will be subject to an 'envirotax escalator', so that their cost increases annually, at well above inflation. This will reduce demand over a five-year timescale, after which all but the most benign garden treatments will be withdrawn.

All other gardening products, however they are sold, will be required to carry a unique 'enviro-code'. Entered online, this will give a detailed 'lifecycle analysis' of that product's costs to the environment. This will include disclosure of the raw materials required to make and run the product (such as oil or minerals), the provenance of those materials, whether they have been ethically sourced, what pollution the manufacture of the product has caused (such as carbon emissions), how far it has travelled, what the environmental implications of using it are, and how recyclable it is at the end of its life. The cost of this scheme will be borne by the industry, and will be subject to rigorous scrutiny. It will bring unprecedented transparency where little currently exists.

While we review the implications of the Climate Change Act 2008, a freeze will be put on all planning applications for large out-of-town, car-dependent garden centres. My government will make a rigorous assessment of whether the monopolisation of gardening by a few large corporations is compatible with the carbon reduction targets enshrined in the Act.

The use of sphagnum peat for making compost will be banned immediately, as its extraction contributes to global warming. A public education campaign will help and advise gardeners during the transition to using composts made from renewable resources. An immediate ban will also apply to patio heaters, and to metaldehyde-based slug pellets.

During the phase-out of oil-derived garden chemicals, my Gardening Government will identify shining examples of earth-friendly gardening, on every scale, in our most densely populated areas. We will then establish a nationwide network of 'growcentres', whose owners will be supported, via our climate taxes, to enable them to showcase ecologically sustainable gardening. In five years' time, almost everyone will have a growcentre within a 30-minute journey of their home, accessible either on foot or by public transport. Each centre will also exist 'virtually' on the internet, and will therefore be a neighbourhood resource accessible 24/7, with mentoring provided by the growcentre champions. For those struggling with the transition away from high-energy, oil-dependent gardening, a free telephone helpline will be established, offering practical advice, as well as emotional support and, where demand exists, anger management counselling.

On a bioregional scale we will seed a network of not-for-profit 'earth centres', which will co-ordinate the collation, curation and propagation of plant varieties uniquely suited to each bioregion. These earth centres will work in synergy with their own families of growcentres, and will become hubs for local seed and plant selection. They will also act as local skill centres. Earth centres will be readily accessible by public transport, and open to all.

These are just some of the policies to be set in motion in the germinating hours of a Gardening Government. From that day on, for our nation, and for all of nature and for all peoples with whom we share this precious earth, things can only get better. When I said that I would put some real plot into politics, I meant it. But it won't just be one plot. It won't be hundreds, not even thousands, but millions of plots, all working with nature to bring us more meaningful, contented lives.

So can we, by turning our hands to the soil, make this gardening nation a deeper shade of green than ever before? Yes, we can. Can we, together, plot by plot, put food gardening at the very core of the ecological imperative to start living more earth-friendly lives?

Yes, my fellow gardeners, we can.

April 2010

MONEY CAN'T BUY LIFE

I DON'T KNOW about you, but I'm wholeheartedly sick of hearing about 'the good life'. Ping goes yet another email newsletter: the motto is 'Making the good life easy!'. In drops another catalogue with its sigh-inducing cover: 'The good life, made easy!'. Yet another emailed advert from a company called Live The Good Life Ltd (proof positive that 'living a good life' is now well and truly commodified; like so much of gardening, it's now something you buy, rather than something you do). Even the government exhorts us to 'get a slice of the good life'. And just when I thought it couldn't get any worse, a telephone conversation deals me the final blow: "Are you living the good life, then?"

Slumped in utter defeat, the best answer I could begrudgingly muster was, "Well, something like that." I quickly steered the conversation on to less frustrating ground, determined not to be characterised as some 21st-century upgrade from the '70s BBC TV sitcom 'The Good Life'. Ingrained as it is in our collective psyche, this programme has an awful lot to answer for. And yet, in a twist of pure irony, deep down it actually has very little in common with the modern blizzard of adverts, messages and ill-conceived articles urging us to 'live the good life – it's easy!'.

For those tender enough in age not to have watched it, 'The Good Life' is about how a couple in their early forties – Tom and Barbara Good – become 'self-sufficient' in suburbia, by growing their own fruit and vegetables, keeping a goat, pigs and chickens, making and mending their own clothes, and running their car on methane. Their conventional middle-class neighbours, Jerry and Margot, look on with disdain at the Goods' many antics as they try to live a more self-reliant and, by definition, 'good' life.

But there are two important aspects of Tom and Barbara's on-screen attempt to live a better life that grate with present-day illusions about what a good life is and how you actually get one. Firstly, 20 minutes into the first episode, Tom gives up his full-time job. Barbara doesn't work, so they face a future with no regular income, although their house is paid for, and they have some savings. Secondly, now they've broken free of the 'rat race', they can do all the things they want to do with total commitment; they have all the time in the world to live a good life.

Despite it being make-believe, at least the Goods understood that the key to living a good life is essentially a combination of much more 'free' time and a healthy acceptance of a reduced income. The two generally go together; if you want to live a better and more creative life, if you want to do more than hock your soul to a five-day working week, if you want to spend more time with family and friends and if – crucially for us, dear reader – you want to become more sufficient in home-grown vegetables and fruits, you need to become time-abundant, while still earning enough to meet basic needs. Being cash-rich and time-poor is no way to grow great veggies.

The sad truth is that the message behind all the current newsletters, adverts and emails that shout to us about how 'easy' the good life is going to be, is that in order to have it, we must spend money – and not just a few quid. One mail-order catalogue has everything we need, apparently, to make our good lives easier, from a wormery for £100 to a wooden compost bin for £145 – and so it is in one glossy catalogue after another.

Now I'm not saying that we should never spend money on our kitchen gardens, but if we want the kind of better life that goes with a growing sense of self-reliance, it follows that we won't actually be able to afford the kind of good lives that today's misguided marketeers are relentlessly trying to flog us. Anyone spinning a 'good life is easy' mantra actually needs to wake up and get a life (good or otherwise). To aspire to a 21st-century-style good life, I'd need to keep working long hours to buy all the stuff that would supposedly make it 'easy' in the free time that, because I'm working so much, I won't actually have. I imagine Tom and Barbara chuckling at the £195 price tag on a 1.4m^2 timber raised bed, before toddling off home to make their own for next to nothing. They had oodles of time to devote to their suburban smallholding, and it was damn hard work. It still is, as anyone who's started a kitchen garden from scratch will attest.

Despite my own efforts at trying to reshape my life (by reducing large debts and the overall cost of day-to-day living, among other things), at times I'm still frustrated by how little time I have to do my own earth-friendly food gardening. I'm self-employed, and enjoy a certain freedom that many crave, so if I feel frustrated, it must be soul-destroying for those who have no control over their working lives, who are trying to juggle long, stressful days with family life, but who are constantly being told that it's easy to have your own slice of the good life. That kind of bunk might make a good soundbite, but it just ain't true. At least not yet.

But there are signs that the grip work has on our lives might be loosening, and there's no doubt that many yearn for something more than the overworking, over-earning and over-consuming lives that are the 21st-century norm. To spur us into contemplating what more satisfying, sustainable lives might actually be like, the New Economics Foundation (NEF), a think-and-do-tank that aims to 'improve quality of life by challenging mainstream thinking on economic, environmental and social issues', recently floated the idea that a 'normal' working week would come, over time, to consist of just 21 hours (or 4.2 hours a day), rather than our culturally ingrained 35 to 40 (or more). The NEF argues that sharing out paid and unpaid time more evenly will help us all to live better, richer lives, as the disparity between the overworked and the underemployed becomes evened out.

The NEF's 21-hour week would also help to tackle 'the interlinked problems of over-consumption, high carbon emissions [we'll earn less, so buy less, so reduce our demands on natural resources], low well-being, entrenched inequality, and the lack of time to live sustainably, to care for each other, and simply to enjoy life.' And it would, of course, give us more time to grow our own food.

Just imagine finishing (or beginning) work at lunchtime every day, and having the rest of the time on your cherished plot. We would have more time to prepare and cook what we'd grown, we'd be much healthier, and we'd be more attuned to the world around us. We'd become more practical and able to make more things ourselves. Just like Tom and Barbara, we'd chuckle at the price tags of gardening stuff sold on the false promise that it will make life 'easy'.

To live 'the good life', we need to fundamentally rebalance our lives in profound, enriching ways that give us much more of that magical ingredient, time. And no catalogue lists that.

May 2010

THE PEAT DELUSION

'IF YOU ARE CONCERNED about green issues, sphagnum moss peat is a renewable resource and growing faster in the northern hemisphere than we are using it in compost.' This quote, from a national newspaper, is deceptively reassuring. But in less time than it takes to say 'peat-free compost', my earth-friendly alarm bells were a-ringing, and it set me on a journey not just into the deep, dark and fascinating world of peat bogs, but into a world of gardening spin inhabited by some dangerous delusions.

Sphagnum moss peat, which is what most peat composts are made from, comes from 'lowland raised bogs', of which only a fraction remain intact in the UK; the rest have succumbed to agriculture, development, and what amounts to the open-cast mining of their peat reserves. Peat, for sure, is wonderful stuff; it's soft, fibrous and crumbly, it smells divine, and almost anything grows brilliantly in it. What else would you expect of a material that's been thousands of years in the making?

But what you might not expect of peat bogs is that they play many vital roles. They're unique, biodiversity-rich habitats; they help protect against flooding and keep our water sweet; they're an irreplaceable archaeological slice through millennia of history; they tell us how our climate has changed over aeons; they form serene, stunning landscapes; and they help regulate the planetary systems which make the thin, fragile layer we live in habitable. But things are changing, and fast.

Since we started burning the 'fossil' fuels coal, oil and gas, we've been dumping carbon dioxide (CO_2), the main greenhouse gas causing climate change, into the atmosphere in ever-increasing amounts. As we increase the CO_2 concentration, it traps more heat energy from the sun – just like your greenhouse warms up until you open the vents.

Climate change is happening, and to slow it and prevent it worsening, we must urgently cut the amount of CO_2 being released through human activities. That's why the government recently launched an 'Act on CO_2' campaign, urging gardeners to use peat-free composts to help reduce our 'carbon footprints' (all of *Which? Gardening*'s latest 'best buy' composts are peat-free). Every time we buy a bag of peat compost, we nudge our climate closer to perilous change.

Buying peat compost is ecologically reckless for a very simple reason. Peat is composed of the dead fragments of mosses, usually sphagnum, and other plants. While these plants are growing, they absorb CO_2 from the air, building it into their tissues. When they die, their remains don't fully rot down in the acidic, waterlogged and airless bog conditions. Given thousands of years, and growing at a rate of 1mm a year, the successive layers of half-decayed, carbon-rich plant material can eventually produce peat deposits up to 12m deep. Given a few hundred million years more, that same peat becomes coal, which is almost pure carbon. So peat is just 'baby' coal, and as such is a fossil fuel that has no place inside any compost bag. Draining peat bogs and then digging up the peat exposes it to the air for the first time, where it decomposes, causing most of the carbon it contains to turn into CO_2. In climate change terms, using peat is the equivalent of burning coal.

How does this relate to filling up your car boot with compost bags? Gardeners account for 70 per cent of UK peat use (commercial growers use the rest). Carbon expert Chris Goodall (www.carboncommentary.com) suggests that the production of a 60-litre bag of 100 per cent sphagnum peat compost could be responsible for releasing up to 50kg of CO_2 into the atmosphere. That's 50kg of CO_2 that was, until the peat was dug up, safely locked away in the largest carbon stores on earth; peat bogs, globally, hold around 550 billion tonnes of carbon. If a million gardeners each use just one bag of peat compost, that's 50,000 tonnes of CO_2; there are 10 to 20 million gardeners in the UK alone. Do the sums.

The government estimates that three million cubic metres of ancient peat are being stripped from our raised bogs each year, causing annual emissions of half a million tonnes of CO_2. But that doesn't include the fact that we import over 50 per cent of the peat we use, so we are effectively 'exporting' those CO_2 emissions and the destruction they trigger, adding ethical concerns to peat extraction's already impressive charge sheet.

These dark, slumbering carbon giants are the most unsung of all our natural 'defences' against climate change, and we disturb them at our peril, but that's exactly what we're being urged to do by some gardening pundits. But why? Do they know something about peat extraction that the rest of us don't? Or are they just so disconnected from nature that they're prepared to callously shove it aside, and unquestioningly believe the misinformation spun by the global peat industry?

The number one myth peddled about peat is that it is a 'renewable' resource, but we know that fossil fuels aren't renewable because they take so long to form – hundreds of millions of years. Yes, peat is still forming, just like coal, oil and gas are, but on an unimaginable timescale. Any natural resource is only renewable, and therefore sustainable, if it is being replenished at the same rate that it's being used. Peat isn't; it 'grows' at a centimetre a decade, and a thousand years' worth of peat is 1m deep. Just because something is renewable doesn't mean it is actually being renewed.

Sleight of hand is also at work. Much is made of how

denuded peat bogs can be 'regenerated'. With effort, this can be done, by allowing water to soak back into the remaining peat and by 'seeding' mosses on to its surface. But it takes a decade or more to get going, and even then the bog doesn't magically recover its former self. It takes thousands of years; we face climate chaos within decades. Imagining that 'regenerated' peat bogs can somehow capture and store the vast amounts of carbon released through their ruination is a dangerous delusion. Each bag of peat compost is responsible for releasing extra CO_2, while destroying peat bogs to fill the bag actually removes an important means of capturing and 'locking up' atmospheric carbon.

Claiming that peat is growing 'faster than we are using it' sounds attractive, but is entirely bogus in terms of UK peat production – that's why 'in the northern hemisphere' slyly creeps in. If it were true, we'd be self-sufficient in peat, with no need to trash others' wild landscapes. In countries like Canada there are vast reserves of peat and, technically, it might well be growing faster than it's being ripped up, but that argument rests on the premise 'there's plenty of it, so let's use it', which treats natural resources as being solely for human consumption. This fallacy comes crashing down, especially in climate terms, because peat is a non-renewable fossil fuel that's releasing CO_2 that was, until the machinery moved in, stored safely away.

All of this is greenwash of a most dangerous variety. Keeping us hooked on peat means that we'll continue, knowingly or otherwise, to play our part in a harmful cycle that's damaging in many different ways. Peat has no place in responsible gardening, and it isn't 'green' in any sense of the word. The best and safest place for it isn't in plastic bags, but in the ground.

June 2010

GARDENING ON THE ROAD

THERE'S QUITE A SINGALONG going on outside my window as I write this. The willow warblers, who've recently arrived back in the wood from warmer climes, are singing their hearts out, preluding spring with the simplest of serenades. Backing vocals include the soothing hum of bees foraging on willow catkins and the faint trickle of the rain-starved stream. After the long winter, laggard bluebells and marsh marigolds are only just stirring, chivvied by the feathered choir to get their skates on.

But there are other, more intrusive sounds too, which interrupt and occasionally drown out this most gentle of nature's compositions. The man-made cacophony ranges from the unsilenced boom of a motorbike to a juggernaut's ground-shaking rumble and the dull humdrum of cars. And there's another: the desperate, foot-to-the-floor whoosh as yet another 'home delivery' van flashes by.

The road across the field from me is fast becoming one of the main arteries of a society that increasingly wants everything to be delivered, and often expects it to arrive within hours of the click of a computer mouse (think groceries). We gardeners, it seems, are no exception, and increasingly share this voracious appetite for stuff to be dropped at our front doors. Everywhere I turn I'm implored to buy: TV shopping channels hard-sell gardening goodies (as well as some dodgy stuff), I'm bombarded daily with junk emails pushing the latest 'stunning' offers, and a relentless stream of catalogues flows through my letterbox. 'Limited availability – ring us now!' 'Exclusive!' 'Call this number to jump the queue!' 'Just one click and you're done!'

You might think it is progress to have everything delivered at a click – the consumer society dream incarnate – but do we gardeners really want or need to go speeding down this road? Have we become so swept up in all this bargain hunting, so desperate for instant gratification, so reliant on our gardens arriving in a cardboard box, that we've somehow lost the real gardening plot?

Don't get me wrong; I love receiving stuff in the post. And by 'the post' I mean delivered by Royal Mail and Parcelforce – you know, those trusty red vans whose drivers know exactly where everyone lives and who unfailingly deliver, rain or shine. I can't deny the enduring thrill that comes with opening a seed order, or a box of vegetable plug plants, or a fruit tree in a big cardboard box. But I am beginning to wonder whether it's time we took our foot off the 24/7 gardening-via-the-letterbox pedal and pondered its implications for the world beyond our own fences, and for the willow warblers outside my window.

Three experiences this spring have rather dented my love of waiting for the arrival of the postie. The first is the tortuous tale of my seed potatoes. Unable to get the varieties I wanted locally and in those handy five-tuber packs, I ordered online from a well-known company. They were destined for growing in large pots under cover as 'ultra-earlies', so imagine my mounting frustration when they took over a month to arrive; they should have been growing when I finally opened the box. And what a job it was to rescue them from the delivery system. Countless emails and, eventually, phone calls and effusive apologies later, the road-weary box arrived, its contents miraculously intact. Who got the 'we tried to deliver' cards through their door I don't know, but it wasn't me.

The mistake I made (apart from having a prat-nav-unfriendly address) is that I didn't check how the order would be sent – but you can't always do that with online ordering, and so my tatties disappeared into delivery limbo. If one of those trusty red vans had got the job, I would have had them within days. I wonder how many times that box whizzed by on the main road, burning fuel, and how much time and energy (and electricity) was expended in sending and receiving emails, and in phone calls between me and the supplier, and between the supplier and the delivery company.

My second dent of faith in buying by post came when another well-known company came under fire for selling carrots as plug plants. Nothing wrong with that, you might think, but the cost of these carrots came out, with postage and packing, at the mind-boggling sum of over £1 per plant. Even the company selling them admitted they were poor value for money and quickly withdrew them.

But that whole rumpus missed the point. What on earth are we doing growing carrots, a root crop, possibly in big heated greenhouses, in plugs of compost, then packaging them up and sending them whizzing around the polluting, fuel-guzzling motorway network? Have we become so distanced from what earth-friendly kitchen gardening is fundamentally about – sowing seeds in soil – that we're happy to encourage ever more gobbling of finite resources, because we can no longer be bothered to open a seed packet? Do we really think that just because everything else in life is now 'deliverable', gardening is too? The folk flogging this kind of stuff were predictably indignant, claiming that they were 'only meeting demand from gardeners'. When did anyone ask you if you wanted carrots by post at £1 a pop?

The third dent is the deepest. One of the current obsessions in my part of North Wales is with 'road improvement', which mostly consists of removing any annoying bends and making roads wider and therefore more 'efficient' (shorthand, almost invariably, for faster and more dangerous). Nothing stands in the way of such 'improvements', be it mighty (or meek) trees, streams, bluebells, ancient rock outcrops or willow warblers; the motorbike, car, coach, juggernaut and, of course, delivery van win every time. As our lives and our gardens become ever more deliverable, nothing must hold them up.

It's a deeply painful dent, too. Not many miles from where I live, on the same main road that noisily overwhelms my songsters, an 'improvement' scheme is underway. The first step was to take a chainsaw to the willow, ash and other trees rooted in the path of progress; decades of steady growth and wildlife-rich habitat were gone in hours. Next, each weeping stump needed only a few mechanised minutes to wrench it from a lush green carpet of wild garlic, which will soon be lost, together with bluebells and marsh marigolds, under hardcore.

There will be no more of nature's spring serenades from the high twigs of that bit of woodland; it's gone forever. Some of the willow warblers lulling me now might even be its evictees. I thought they were singing in celebration of the sheer joy of spring, but listening more carefully, it could well be a lament.

But not to worry; with the bends nicely smoothed out, all those haring vans – assuming they know where they're going – will now be able to get our gardens to us that bit quicker.

July 2010

KICKING THE HABIT

HERE'S A QUESTION for you: what does the catastrophic oil spill in the Gulf of Mexico (still underway as I write this) have to do with your garden? And while you're pondering that, try this: how much of the materials, equipment and gadgetry that make your kitchen gardening possible is made from a dark liquid just like that gushing from 1,500m (5,000ft) down on the ocean floor? Here's a clue to get you started, whether you're of an organic disposition or not: rather a lot.

The ecological disaster unfolding in the Gulf of Mexico has permeated the news for months, ever since the BP-run 'ultra-deepwater semi-submersible oil rig' Deepwater Horizon suffered a massive explosion in late April, and sank a few days later, with the loss of 11 lives. During the rig's collapse, pipes carrying oil became damaged, and several subsequent attempts to plug or contain the leak failed. Since then, anywhere between 5,000 and 25,000 barrels (estimates vary) of crude oil a day have continued, after aeons of slumber, to spew from beneath the seabed.

Soon after the rig sank, slicks of dark liquid began to appear on the ocean surface and drift toward the ecologically fragile coastlines of Alabama, Louisiana and Mississippi in the southern USA. The worst man-made oil industry disaster in American history began to unfold and, by early June, was clearly visible from space.

I was in my greenhouse the day the Deepwater Horizon

caught fire, sowing seeds in some much-used plastic pots and various plastic cell trays acquired over the years. The peat-free compost I was using was scooped from a plastic bag, and I wrote names and sowing dates on yellowing, much-scrubbed plastic labels. It was then that I asked myself the same two questions I've just asked you.

Here's my answer to the second one: plant pots, multi-cell trays, some plug plant packaging, a fading plastic watering can, compost bins, a hosepipe, a hand sprayer, fruit cage netting, some fleece and insect mesh, a plant food container, some buckets, ground cover fabric, shade netting, garden twine, a couple of Tubtrugs, a water tank, a birdfeeder, some bed edging, some old polytunnel covering, a 'patio bag', and numerous empty compost bags. Granted, some are 'recycled' – the bed edging is made from plastic milk bottles and the water tank once contained orange juice – but all of the stuff on my list ultimately derives from one ancient substance: oil.

How did you get on? If you're definitely not of an organic disposition, I'd wager that you can confidently tick 'all of the above', and then some. How about adding insecticides, fungicides and weedkillers to your list? What about synthetic chemical fertilisers and plant foods? Almost without exception, all of these are derived from that dark stuff oozing from the seabed. And don't forget the packaging; the worrying trend toward ever more elaborate and over-packaged garden 'convenience chemicals' only adds to our growing addiction to crude. Some even have oh-so-handy sprayers with pumps powered by batteries (we're too lazy to even squeeze our fingers together any more).

Let's face it: in gardening terms, organic or otherwise, we're up to our necks in the stuff. If we could wave a magic wand and turn all of the oil-derived materials in our gardens and allotments back into crude oil, our plots would be plastered with dark and smelly gunk. Like me, you have probably never seen, smelt or touched an oil spill in the flesh, but looking at pictures of the Deepwater Horizon disaster, especially through the impassive eye of an orbiting satellite, and then glancing around my patch, reminds me of gardening's often painfully high ecological price tag.

For many gardeners, even us supposedly earth-friendly organic ones, kicking the oil habit is going to take some effort. If we don't do it voluntarily, driven by a growing sense of obligation to respect the beleaguered life-support systems around us, we'll end up doing it the cold turkey way. Those of us growing organically can take some comfort from knowing that we're now through the worst; you might say we are 'recovering gardeners'.

If you've kicked the habit completely, if you're tending a flourishing and abundant food-bearing plot which depends on barely a drop of fresh oil being extracted, give yourself a pat on the back (and let me know how you do it). But if you are still getting your oil-derived fix, if you are in thrall to chemical-pushing gardening pundits-cum-dealers, don't fret; it's never too late to join an organic recovery programme.

Although growing organically spares us the worst shakes and shivers of addiction recovery, most of us will have some way to go before we're completely tremor-free. But the rewards, both for ourselves and for the world around us, are priceless. By weaning ourselves off oil, we can, as gardeners, send a powerful signal down the supply chain that reduces demand for it (and for the other 'fossil fuels', coal and natural gas).

One of the main reasons for the spill in the Gulf of Mexico is that as demand for oil continues to rise, easily extractable oil supplies are getting harder to find, forcing oil companies to search for ever more hard-to-reach reserves. Piping oil from 5,000ft down on the sea floor is a dangerous, precarious business, with dire consequences when it goes wrong. Reducing demand for oil decreases the urgency to exploit increasingly risk-laden reserves.

By cutting back on all 'new' oil coming into our gardens, by using pots until they are on their last legs, by keeping fleece and insect mesh until it's threadbare, by patching up leaky hoses, and by simply choosing oil-less stuff, we might just lessen the risk of another Deepwater Horizon. If this smacks of being a futile gesture when you look around your own plot, try multiplying it up by tens of millions of gardeners the world over; together, we would make a real difference.

Will reducing or cutting off the flow of new oil-based stuff into our gardens be so bad? We might get the shakes at the thought of no more fleece or insect mesh, but I'm sure we could hold it together sufficiently to squidge cabbage white butterfly eggs and hand-pick any caterpillars, while bumping up our companion planting to bring in beneficial insects.

Better still, perhaps those who make these wonderfully useful materials might actually get around to ensuring they are fully and easily recyclable; whatever you think of plastic, it's a durable resource that can be sent around in a virtuous cycle indefinitely. And what's to stop us insisting – nay, demanding – that any really indispensable organic gardening stuff be made from oil that's already 'in the system', and that it just keeps going round and round?

They may be far apart, but our gardens and the dark, growing slick glinting in the sun off the USA's southern coast are inextricably linked. Anyone for rehab?

August 2010 – *Winner of the 2010 Garden Media Guild Environmental Award*

DROUGHT OF GOOD SENSE

VICTIMISED, THREATENED and dealt a cruel blow by a heartless world; it sure is tough out there if you're a gardener (especially one growing food). Woe are we, especially when it comes to watering our gardens and allotments. Our greatest tormentors, it seems, are those nasty, profit-glugging and leakage-prone water companies. When reservoirs begin drying up and river levels start falling, when fish start suffocating, and stream beds start cracking, they strike fear deep into our horticultural hearts by threatening to ban the use of hosepipes for garden watering.

Cue then a veritable flood of heartbreaking headlines; tales of how we gardening folk are being browbeaten, punished, treated unfairly and discriminated against. You can't help but feel for us poor, embattled gardeners, especially when reading, from the Horticultural Trades Association (HTA) – the UK's main gardening industry body – of how we face being forced to 'neglect and kill off valuable plants' at the behest of water companies. Our fate, it seems, is to stand by and watch, our arms wearied beyond repair by the terrible, inhuman task of having to use watering cans to convey the life-giving stuff to our plants, as our crops shrivel in the merciless sun. Oh please, try pulling the other end of the emotional hosepipe; I don't buy a word of it.

It's true that less than one per cent of all the fresh water on earth is readily available for human use (the rest is either seawater or frozen). It's true that this year the UK has seen the second driest six-month period in 50 years. It's true that finite supplies of fresh water are under increasing pressure from growing industrial, agricultural, horticultural and indeed domestic demand (including garden use). It's true that some gardeners have not a clue how to respect water and use it wisely. It's true that some folk flogging gardening products don't have any understanding of the words 'wise watering' (one press release I received, in the middle of the six-month dry spell, recommended a lawn sprinkler as an essential bit of 'waterwise' kit...). And it's almost a cert that most of the population, gardeners or not, have little inkling of where the stuff gushing from their taps comes from, or of the environmental price tag it carries.

But I fail to see any grounds for anointing gardeners with their current levels of victimhood. This is as much to do with a yawning knowledge gap among gardeners old and new, and a lazy, it-will-always-be-there mentality, as it is with our gardening industry, as usual, protecting its own vested and ecologically tepid interests.

It's true, too, that the prolonged dry spell earlier this year took many a gardener by surprise, myself included. One June evening stopped me in my tracks. I knew something was missing, but it was a shock to realise that it was the glug of the small stream running below my garden, which had fallen silent for the first time in the seven years I've walked alongside it (it was all the more astonishing because this is North Wales, and the stream is frequently transformed into a raging torrent). Predictably, things began to improve as this article went together; nothing opens the heavenly floodgates quite like writing about hosepipe bans...

Although my disappearing stream took me by surprise, it didn't have me instantly joining the HTA's ranks of oppressed, water-deprived gardeners; my 1,500-litre (330-gallon) exorange juice water tank saw to that. When July's downpours finally came, I was using water, mostly for the greenhouse, from a still half-full tank. It's rather hard to feel victimised when you're drowning in smugness – not to mention deep satisfaction – at having taken responsibility for meeting your garden's water needs without needing to turn on a mains tap.

Earth-friendly organic kitchen gardeners know all about water, and learn to respect it. We peer into the end of a hosepipe and understand what's going on at the other end of the supply line. We know that extracting fresh water from rivers, streams and lakes has an impact on aquatic ecosystems, and that drawing water from underground aquifers can lower water tables and deplete supplies of 'fossil water'. We know that building dams can drown natural habitats and, in some parts of the world, displace human communities, and that purifying water and then delivering it to our homes is an energy-intensive business.

But what we know and learn most of all is that there's plenty you can do to break dependency on energy-intensive tap water, none of which is rocket science. Improving the moisture-retaining ability of our soil with organic matter, harvesting as much rainwater as we can and storing it in the biggest containers we can afford and find space for, mulching like mad, reducing container growing to a minimum, and only watering when it's absolutely necessary, are our 'big five'.

Don't expect to see or hear much from the HTA (or any other part of the gardening industry) on these biggies. I don't recall a torrent of press releases during the recent six-month dry spell urging gardeners to invest in water butts and tanks so that they can reduce their reliance on tap water (probably because garden centres simply hadn't stocked up on them for 2010, so there would have been no sales to be had). Soil improvement, harvesting rainwater, mulches and common-sense watering are not big sellers (and don't keep you hooked on irrigation gadgetry).

The rub at the heart of this manufactured victimhood is this: most modern watering systems rely on mains tap water, especially its pressure, to work. To fill a watering can, you place it under a water butt tap, fill it, then take it to the plants that need it. To water with an automatic system, you not only need a spaghetti-like network of pipes and tubing, non-return valves, filters, and probably a battery-powered timer, but it must also be connected to a mains tap. When a hosepipe ban is enacted, doing this becomes an offence (as does any garden watering using a hosepipe). No one would dispute that if tap water must be used, then using a 'precision' watering system is a better option than spraying tap water willy-nilly from the end of a hosepipe.

The fear of hosepipe bans, which is being projected on to gardeners, is felt much more keenly by those who make and sell garden watering equipment; the possibility that we might stop watering our plants so much, and start looking for far more eco-friendly, non-tap water ways to do it, is a very deep fear. The HTA talks about 'confusion amongst consumers', how 'hosepipe bans deter people from planting and gardening', how this 'negatively impacts on garden centres... in times of drought', and how, in 2006, it cost the gardening industry £12m in lost sales.

As water supplies become more stretched, hosepipe bans will inevitably become more frequent; they're something that all gardeners will ultimately have to adapt to. Central to that is using the 'big five' ways to make the most of the free and renewable rainwater falling on our gardens and allotments. And the more we do that, the less likely it is that we'll be co-opted as unwitting and convenient 'victims' whenever the rivers run low.

September 2010

COMPOST CRISIS

WHEN WELL-KNOWN gardening pundits start proclaiming just how 'awful' it is that children should get their hands dirty when using 'filthy' potting compost, you know that something's going seriously wrong in the world of compost manufacturing. Like many gardeners who temporarily suspended their disbelief at the revelation that compost makes your fingers dirty, I pondered, though only for a millisecond, whether a non-hand-dirtying potting mix might exist. Alas, no one has yet slit open a bag of 'clean' potting compost, and if there's any sanity left in the world, we never will.

The only clue you need as to why this bizarre claim came about is that the said compost was a peat-free mixture that, in one school garden, had given comparatively poor results. To add to the 'awfulness', our pundit laments how they picked thorny twigs and bits of glass from other peat-reduced compost mixes, and how this terrifying combo of alien fragments and dirty hands would scare children away from ever gardening again. Their 'solution', of course, is to only use peat-based seed and potting composts, even though digging up peat, a 'fossil' source of carbon dioxide, contributes directly to global warming and destroys wildlife-rich bog habitats. You can imagine the classroom confusion: the gardening expert is telling the teachers to use peat compost (presumably to save on hand-washing), while the teachers are explaining to their pupils how using peat is helping to worsen climate change...

This is just one example of how low some gardening commentators now stoop in order to denigrate any compost mixture that's not pumped full of peat. The peat mining industry is long past its ecological sell-by date, but that isn't going to prevent the pro-peat pundits from using every trick in the book to keep us hooked until they've flogged their last bag of the stuff.

It's also just one symptom of a crisis now unfolding at the heart of the compost-making industry. But this is no single-issue crisis; its roots are deep, and spreading. Its key, intertwined components are, in no particular order: ignorance and confusion, lack of information, disinformation, spin, 'cheap as chips' expectations, selfishness, limp gardening journalism – and turning of a blind eye to scientific reality.

Let's get the 'scientific' bit straight. When you dig up peat, a non-renewable 'fossil' substance on a par with coal, oil and natural gas, to make compost, it dries out and the carbon it previously stored safely in the ground is released as carbon dioxide, the main 'greenhouse gas' driving global climate change. Mining peat also destroys wetland ecosystems which, when left intact, actually absorb and safely lock away carbon from the air – they're some of the earth's most important carbon 'sinks'.

In contrast, making peat-free compost from 'green waste' (collected via household wheelie bins) diverts organic materials – anything from old brassica stalks to lawn mowings – from going to the 'tip' and then to a landfill site, where they get buried in the ground. There, in the compressed, compacted and airless conditions, they rot down and produce methane, another greenhouse gas, but one 25 times more powerful than carbon dioxide. So by making compost primarily from plant remains, we're both removing the need to use climate-altering peat and avoiding methane production.

It's true that when plants rot down, either in your compost

bin or in those big, steaming windrows you see on the edge of town, they release much of the carbon they stored while they were growing. But they only release what they absorbed from the air in the first place; when we dig up peat we're actually adding extra carbon to the atmosphere that was previously locked away in 'fossil' form (plus any arising from processing, bagging, transporting and selling it). Making peat-free compost isn't drawback-free. Energy is still burned to gather the raw materials, to turn the heaps, and then to transport the finished product, but if the composting process takes place close to where the raw materials are sourced, its 'carbon footprint' starts to look a lot lighter than that of peat-based composts.

So what about the fragments of glass, twigs and other bits and bobs that doubtless do appear in bags of peat-free from time to time? When you're collecting green waste on a vast scale some contamination is unavoidable, and some 'bits' are inevitably going to thwart even the most rigorous screening process. Peat-based composts do tend to be free of unwanted detritus, but the real test is whether our awareness of the ecological consequences of using peat can be trumped by the annoyance of finding a few 'bits' when we open a bag of peat-free. A few 'bits' (bar glass, which is a no-no in anyone's book) are, surely, a small price to pay for climate-friendly compost?

The perceived underperformance of peat-free composts is another line of attack favoured by the pro-peat brigade. Unfortunately, peat-free compost is subject to a phenomenon afflicting every aspect of life: you rarely hear good news. The letters pages of gardening magazines seemingly abound with horror stories of how awful peat-free and peat-reduced composts are; it'd be a rare reader who would take the trouble to put pen to paper to sing the praises of peat-free (although *Which? Gardening* did award 'best buys' to three peat-free container composts earlier this year).

Even gardening journalists are happy to jump on the peat-free-bashing bandwagon. One editor recently trumpeted how they would rather not play Russian roulette with their plants, and would be sticking with peat-based compost because they couldn't watch their plants die. Gardening success, it seems, must come at any price – even if it means playing Russian roulette with the climate itself.

But the chief catalyst of our compost crisis is us; we just don't pay enough for the stuff. For many years all we've heard is 'buy two, get one free' or 'three bags for a tenner'. Our resulting mindset, ably massaged by a profit-hungry gardening industry, has forced the manufacturers of peat-free compost to get it down to a rock-bottom price, 'cheap as chips'. Is it any wonder that some gardeners get less than perfect results with peat-free when all they're spending on it is a few quid? Nurserymen who use peat-free compost pay considerably more for a superior, reliable product, to ensure that they stay in business. It's about time we did, too, not only to ensure that our food mile-cutting kitchen garden crops succeed, but also to avoid the climate chaos that's already wiping out crops in distant plots, less pampered than ours.

Our compost crisis isn't going to be solved by some silver bullet fired into the heart of the compost-making industry. As earth-friendly gardeners we can do our bit to give climate-friendly compost a leg up, by being prepared to pay a realistic price for top-quality peat-free mixes that are consistent, reliable and – hopefully – free of 'bits'.

It might come as a jolt when the barcode's scanned at the checkout, but the peat-free bleep will be as nothing compared to the ecological alarm bells set off by scanning a bag of peat-based multipurpose.

November 2010

ALWAYS ASK QUESTIONS

ALTHOUGH I DON'T NORMALLY make a habit of getting folk to fall off their seats, I'm developing rather a taste for it, if not an impish craving. I know I've scored a real 'hit' when the prelude to the seat-dislodging moment is that delicious few seconds of stunned silence, often garnished with bewilderment. So what powers do I possess to bring about these illuminating moments? Why, nothing more earth-shattering than the nous to ask questions – and to remember to keep on asking them.

They're powerful things, questions. Asking them sometimes brings discomfort and disbelief – for both the questioner and the questioned – but they can also enlighten and inform, broaden minds and change behaviour. Questions can be awkward, funny, complicated, difficult, interesting, loaded, boring, double-edged, revealing, spiked – I could go on – but by far the most effective are the straightforward ones, which give their recipient zero wriggle-room.

A recent and overwhelmingly positive experience with a manufacturer of top-class garden polytunnels was marred only by the discovery that this firm had forgotten to ask itself a fundamental and important question. That I was 'the first person to ask that' reveals a lot about how little thought some makers of gardening materials and equipment have given to what eventually happens to the things they sell us – and how disconnected so much of the gardening industry still is from a truly holistic approach to sustainable living and gardening.

It all started so well. I used the firm's website to request a paper copy of their catalogue (you can't mull over acquiring a new polytunnel unless you've a cuppa to hand and there's dirt under your nails), and it arrived promptly the next day. It was all good, info-packed and impressive stuff, and when I was ready I could play around online with different dimensions (and prices) to my heart's content. A week or so later a friendly call from the tunnel maker, to see if I had any questions (more soft than hard sell), had me mentally nodding them top marks for follow-up customer service.

And yes, I did have a very straightforward question, one which, I explained, hadn't been answered either by their catalogue or their website. "When it comes to the end of its life, can the plastic cover be recycled?" Cue the delicious momentary silence and the gentle creak of a wobbling chair. "Err... I don't know. I don't think anyone has ever asked before – do you mind holding on while I ask a colleague?" I rank falling-off-chair moments by how long it takes for the emergency office confab to come up with an answer. This one scored pretty high.

The answer was a kind of 'yes'. With a little coaxing from me, the tunnel maker suggested that the best way to recycle a tired cover would be through one of the large plastics recycling banks found in car parks. Sensing they were teetering on their chair edges, I dealt a final, irresistible blow. "Have you thought about putting some recycling information in your catalogue?" Wham! "Well, I'll certainly pass your suggestion on..." came the buttock-smarting reply. I was as stunned to find they'd clearly not considered this aspect of the 'afterlife' of their polytunnels as they were to be asked about it. Questions, eh?

One question often leads to another. Thinking five to ten years ahead (when the plastic cover will be on its way out), my next question was to my local authority's recycling department. "Can the old plastic cover from a garden polytunnel be recycled?" This answer, after an initial "I'll just check", was a more solid 'yes', but I was advised that it would be better to put it (clean, dry and folded) in a car-park plastics bank, or take it to the local recycling centre (that's 'tip' to the unbothered throw-it-alls), rather than try to get it into a kerbside collection box. Although bereft of both stunned silence and any prospect of that craved falling-off-chair moment, I was at least reassured that when I'm done with it, a used polytunnel cover (essentially a dollop of refined oil) will at least stand a good chance of going on to be turned into something else.

I'm often told I must live a tortured, fretful life, worrying about every last detail, constantly questioning where something has come from, what it's made of, who made it and where, how it got here and – perhaps the most important question of all – what'll happen to it when it's no longer up to the job. That could well be true, but I blame my sometimes restless nights squarely on being an earth-friendly organic gardener. We are, after all, a rare breed: folk who veer toward a seemingly irrational despair at the very thought of chucking stuff out, instead always finding another use for it, and who are equally and increasingly wary and questioning when acquiring new gardening stuff. Standing in the yard at my 'recycling' centre, with perfectly good gardening stuff showering into waiting skips headed for landfill, I feel I'm in truly alien territory.

If we're to stand any chance of evolving into the greener and more 'sustainable' human society we keep hearing so much about, one which is 'green' from our gardens upwards, where we use limited natural resources with care and respect, we all need to start doing a lot more joined-up thinking, not to mention a heap more joined-up gardening. The big problem at present, from which the gardening world isn't immune, is that there are still far too many rather vital dots needing to be joined up – as my polytunnel experience showed.

Did my clearly unexpected question make a difference? So far, it seems not; the polytunnel firm I had falling off its chair still carries no advice, at the time of writing, on its website (nor, I assume, in its paper catalogue) about recycling an old tunnel cover. I can only speculate as to why; perhaps my suggestion was never passed on, or perhaps it was and just got ignored. Or maybe the reason is that it was only a single, disconcerting question lost amid an incoming tidal wave of customer orders.

But what if they started to receive dozens, hundreds, perhaps even thousands of questions about whether their polytunnel covers could be recycled – would that make a difference? Would the effort be mustered to add some recycling advice to their otherwise splendid info packs? Might an avalanche of straightforward questions from us 'end users' bring about much less in the way of lazy cradle-to-grave thinking by manufacturers, and far more cradle-to-cradle farsightedness? Could we see manufacturers thinking more responsibly about the materials they use, so that recycling becomes second nature – an integral part of the deal when we buy more or less anything? Will we one day be cladding our polytunnels with covers actually made from pre-loved plastic, which the original supplier will happily take back when it reaches the end of its life with us?

We don't, of course, need to restrict ourselves to polytunnel covers. There are plenty of other areas where we, as eco-savvy gardeners, can have those who supply us with our gardening gear falling from their seats in stunned silence. All we need to do is keep popping simple, straightforward questions. But be warned – it can become addictive.

So what are you waiting for? Go ask.

December 2010

A good read?

Without reviews from readers like you, it's hard to spread the word about independently published books like this one, and help them reach more readers.

Leaving an honest review at an online bookseller only takes a few minutes and it doesn't have to be long or complicated; just a few sentences sharing with other gardeners what you liked about *Digging Deep in the Garden: Book Four*, and what they might like about it themselves, is incredibly valuable to me.

In truth, very few readers leave book reviews. Adding yours helps me, as an independent, self-publishing writer, to sell more earth-friendly gardening books – and to create new ones.

Thank you.

Why not enjoy another good read?

To be among the first to hear about other publications from Earth-friendly Books, you can sign up, safely and securely, for my occasional newsletter (sent by email) by visiting www.earthfriendlygardener.net and following the newsletter sign-up instructions.

Comments or observations on my books are always welcome. Please email john@earthfriendlygardener.net, or join me on Twitter @earthFgardener

About John Walker

John Walker is an award-winning gardening and environmental author, writer, blogger and micropublisher with 40 years' experience in practical gardening, teaching and the garden media. He grew up in the countryside, caught the gardening bug while still at school, and trained at Birmingham Botanical Gardens, Cambridge University Botanic Garden and the Royal Botanic Gardens Kew, where he was awarded the Kew Diploma in Horticulture. He is also a qualified teacher. John was features/deputy editor of *Garden Answers* magazine and contributing editor of *Kitchen Garden*.

John writes about organic, earth-friendly gardening for newspapers and magazines, including *The Guardian* and *The Daily Telegraph*, and for the Royal Horticultural Society's journal *The Garden*. His collections of cage-rattling essays, *Digging Deep in the Garden*, explore gardening's place in nature. A new edition of *Weeds: An Organic, Earth-friendly Guide to their Identification, Use and Control* was published in 2016. John's *How to Create an Eco Garden: The Practical Guide to Greener, Planet-friendly Gardening* was shortlisted for the 2012 Garden Media Guild Practical Book of the Year. He wrote *The Bed and Border Planner*, edited *A Gardeners' Guide to Annuals*, and contributed to the *Garden Organic Encyclopedia of Organic Gardening*. John has won the Garden Media Guild Environmental Award three times, and has been shortlisted for Gardening Journalist of the Year three times.

John is slowly making a new earth- and climate-friendly garden from a once bracken-riddled hillside at his edge-of-woodland home in Snowdonia, North Wales.

Visit John's website www.earthfriendlygardener.net, follow him on Twitter @earthFgardener, or email john@earthfriendlygardener.net

Roll call of earth-friendly gardening honour

Thank you to everyone who supported the
first edition of this book:

Alison Quinsey
Alwen and Frank Gardner
Betty Dawes
Betty Walker
Carole Shorney
CherryAid Ltd
Cherry Lavell
Freda Maxfield
Hannah Roberts
Jane Gleghorn
Jane Jamieson
Jayne Childs
Jo Latimer
Jon Knight
Judith Conroy
June Williams
Liz Till
Maryline Leese
Nick Dakin Elliot
Nicky Kyle
Patricia Handley
Paul, Rachel and Dougal Mather
Peter Snazell
Phil Latham
Terry Wells
Tom Rigby

Lightning Source UK Ltd.
Milton Keynes UK
UKHW011226121020
371443UK00002B/426

9 780993 268373